SEP 1 2 2006	**DATE DUE**		

Protecting Habitats

PROTECTING
Polar
Regions

Anita Ganeri

GARETH**STEVENS**
PUBLISHING
A Member of the WRC Media Family of Companies

Please visit our web site at: www.garethstevens.com
For a free color catalog describing Gareth Stevens Publishing's list of high-quality books
and multimedia programs, call 1-800-542-2595 (USA) or 1-800-387-3178 (Canada).
Gareth Stevens Publishing's fax: (414) 332-3567.

Library of Congress Cataloging-in-Publication Data

Ganeri, Anita, 1961
    Protecting polar regions / Anita Ganeri. — North American ed.
      p. cm. — (Protecting habitats)
    Includes index.
    ISBN 0-8368-4993-0 (lib. bdg.)
    1. Natural history—Polar regions—Juvenile literature. 2. Habitat conservation—Juvenile literature.
    I. Title. II. Series.
    QH84.1.G36 2005
    577.5'86—dc22   2005042624

This North American edition first published in 2006 by
Gareth Stevens Publishing
A Member of the WRC Media Family of Companies
330 West Olive Street, Suite 100
Milwaukee, WI 53212 USA

This U.S. edition copyright © 2006 by Gareth Stevens, Inc. Original edition copyright © 2004 by Franklin Watts.
First published in Great Britain in 2004 by Franklin Watts, 96 Leonard Street, London, EC2A 4XD, UK.

Designer: Rita Storey
Editor: Sarah Ridley
Art Director: Jonathan Hair
Editor-in-Chief: John C. Miles
Picture Research: Susan Mennell
Map and graph artwork: Ian Thompson

Gareth Stevens Editor: Gini Holland
Gareth Stevens Cover Design: Dave Kowalski

Photo credits (t=top)
Klaus Andrews/Still Pictures: 25; Fred Bruemmer/Still Pictures: 12
Stuart Donachie/Ecoscene: 16, 23; Bryan Knox/Ecoscene: 14
NASA/Ecoscene: 21; Graham Neden/Ecoscene: 4–5
Fritz Polking/Ecoscene: front cover (t), 10, 15
Galen Rowell/Corbis: 1, front cover and 19; Kjell Sandved/Ecoscene: 22
Roland Seitre/Still Pictures: 8; Roger Tidman/FLPA: 7
Robert Weight/Ecoscene: 24; Mike Whittle/Ecoscene: 26

Printed in the United States of America

1 2 3 4 5 6 7 8 9 09 08 07 06 05

CONTENTS

What Are the Polar Regions?

Lying at both ends of Earth, the two polar regions — the Arctic and Antarctic — make up about 8 percent of the world's surface. Covered in vast expanses of ice and snow, and battered by gale-force winds, the Poles are among Earth's most isolated and hostile habitats.

The Arctic

The Arctic is centered on the North Pole, which marks the northern end of the Earth's axis. The region includes the Arctic Ocean and the northern parts of North America, Europe, and Asia, together with the island of Greenland. Some geographers describe the area as bordered by the Arctic Circle, an

This view of snow-covered mountains in Antarctica shows the remote and barren nature of the polar environment.

4

Today, the polar regions are under serious threat. Pollution, drilling for oil, mining, overfishing and illegal fishing, tourism, and other human activities are damaging these fragile habitats and putting the people, plants, and animals that depend on these regions at risk. Many scientists are worried that global warming and holes in the ozone are causing climate changes in the polar regions that will have a domino effect on the rest of the world. This book looks at some of these problems and the measures being taken to protect these special places and safeguard them for the future.

imaginary line drawn around the northern-most part of the Earth. The name Arctic comes from the ancient Greek word for *bear* and refers to the constellation of the Great Bear which appears in the northern sky.

The Antarctic

The name Antarctic means "opposite the bear." It is used to describe the region around the South Pole, which marks the southern end of Earth's axis. The region includes the continent of Antarctica and the sea around it, which is called the Southern Ocean. It is bordered by the Antarctic Circle. The fifth largest continent, Antarctica is also the most isolated. Its nearest neighbor is South America, which is about 621 miles (1,000 kilometers) away. The last continent to be mapped, people did not set foot in Antarctica and explore until almost 200 years ago.

Polar Cold

Both of the polar regions are among the coldest places on Earth. The Poles are so cold because the Sun's rays hit them at an angle and are spread out over a wide area. Additionally, the rays have to take a longer route through Earth's atmosphere to reach the Poles than they do at, for example, the equator, and much of their heat is absorbed on the way. The vast covering of ice at the Poles also helps keep them cold. Instead of soaking up the Sun's rays, white ice reflects most of the heat back into space. This is called the albedo effect: Light colors reflect heat away, while dark colors absorb heat.

In Arctic Greenland, winter temperatures plummet to below –40° Fahrenheit (–40° Celsius). The Antarctic is even colder, with an average winter temperature of –76° F (–60°C). Even in summer, temperatures inland rarely rise above 5° F (–15°C.) The lowest air temperature ever recorded on Earth was measured at –128.56° F (–89.2°C) at Russia's Vostok research station in Antarctica on July 21, 1983. Not only the coldest continent, Antarctica is also the windiest, with wind speeds of over 186 miles (300 km) per hour. At both polar regions, the wind chill factor makes it feel colder than it actually is. Wind chill is a temperature calculation that combines the factors of wind speed at a height of five feet with air temperature while assuming zero sunlight.

The Ends of the Earth

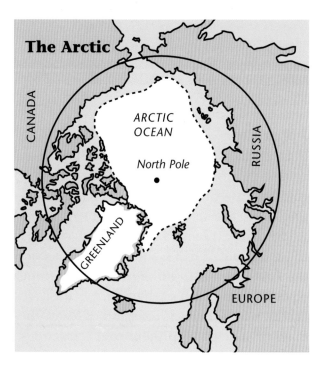

The Arctic

CANADA

ARCTIC OCEAN

North Pole

GREENLAND

RUSSIA

EUROPE

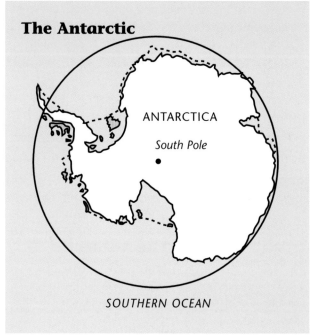

The Antarctic

ANTARCTICA

South Pole

SOUTHERN OCEAN

The Arctic and Antarctic have many things in common. Both polar regions are cold and icy, with short, cool summers and long, dark winters. Both are remote, largely barren, and hostile. Yet there are big differences between the polar regions, too.

Frozen Ocean

There is no solid land at the North Pole itself. It lies in the middle of the Arctic Ocean which, for most of the year, is covered in a layer of permanently frozen ice up to about 10 feet (3 meters) thick.

Covering about 5,405,430 square miles (14 million sq km), the Arctic Ocean is the world's smallest ocean and is almost entirely surrounded by continents and islands. These include Greenland, the world's largest island. Much of Greenland is covered by a huge

sheet of ice up to 1.86 miles (3 km) thick. The low-lying, ice-free land around the edges of the Arctic Ocean is called tundra, which comes from the Finnish word for *treeless plain*. Strong, icy winds sweep this region, making it impossible for tall trees to grow. Beneath the surface, the ground is permanently frozen. This permafrost can be up to 656 yards (600 m) thick; even in summer only the top few inches (centimeters) thaw. The tundra is dotted with lakes and marshes because the permafrost stops water from draining away.

Icy Continent

In contrast to the Arctic, the Antarctic is a frozen continent surrounded by sea, with the South Pole roughly in the middle of it. The continent of Antarctica covers about 5,405,430 square miles (14 million sq km), as big as the United States and Mexico combined. It is also the highest continent on

MIDNIGHT SUN

For several months during the summer, the Sun never sets in the polar regions. During winter, the opposite happens and there is 24-hour darkness.

As the Earth orbits the Sun, the Earth spins once on its axis every 24 hours. The Earth also tilts on its axis in such a way that one hemisphere leans toward the Sun while the other hemisphere leans away. When it is summer at the North Pole, it is winter at the South. So, during the time when the North Pole has constant daylight and the Sun shines at midnight, the South Pole is cloaked in darkness and the Sun never rises above the horizon. Then the seasons are reversed.

Earth, with an average height above sea level of 7,546 feet (2,300 m). Over 99 percent of Antarctica is capped by ice. Buried beneath the ice are mountains and volcanoes, including the active volcano, Mount Erebus. The tops of the highest mountain chains stick up above the ice. Less than 1 percent of Antarctica is free from ice and snow. Much ice-free land is made up of vast areas of bare rock called dry valleys. Technically, Antarctica counts as a desert because it receives only 6 inches (150 millimeters) of rain or snow each year. Amazingly, the dry valleys near McMurdo Sound in southern Antarctica have had no rain for two million years.

The Arctic Ocean is frozen for most of the year.

Why Are the Poles Important?

At first sight, the polar regions may seem desolate, ice-bound wastelands. Nonetheless, because of their position at the ends of the Earth, they are vitally important to our world. For example, the Poles help control weather systems and provide rich environments for scientific exploration.

Science Laboratory

Because they are so clean and unspoiled, the Arctic and Antarctic are exciting places for scientific research that cannot be carried out anywhere else on Earth. At both Poles, scientists are using the latest, cutting-edge technology to find out as much as possible about polar geology, climate, and wildlife.

Research carried out at the Poles is not only important for life on planet Earth. Scientists in Antarctica have found colonies of bacteria flourishing there in some of the harshest conditions known. The bacteria live in pockets of water buried 6.6 feet (2 m) beneath the ice. They use tiny amounts of sunlight, carbon dioxide, and minerals for nourishment. In winter, they can even survive when the water freezes solid. These findings have made scientists wonder about the possibility of life existing at the polar ice caps on Mars, where the cold, dry conditions are similar to those in Antarctica.

The Arctic and Antarctic provide unique natural laboratories for scientific research because they are the last two unspoiled wildernesses left on Earth.

Global Climate

Because the Poles are cold, they play a vital part in regulating the world's weather and climate. The cold, icy ground at the Poles means that the air above it is always cold. This cold air sinks and spreads out from the Poles, creating an area of high pressure. Meanwhile, warm air at the equator rises, causing an area of low pressure. Air moves from high to low pressure, causing the world's circulation of winds. The winds spread heat around Earth, regulating its temperature. Where cold polar air meets the warm tropical air, this confrontation creates weather systems and storms. Without the Poles, planet Earth would not have these weather systems.

Polar weather is so important for the rest of the world that it is a major area of study for scientists. Antarctica alone runs about one hundred weather stations. The information collected there is sent to weather forecasting centers all over the world. Scientists think that the world is getting warmer, putting the polar ice caps at risk. If the ice melts, it could raise sea levels by many feet (meters) and spell disaster for low coastal areas (see page 20).

Polar Resources

It is thought that large amounts of precious oil, gas, and minerals lie buried beneath the Poles. In the Arctic, people have already begun to exploit these resources by building oil pipelines and refineries. Many scientists are worried that this will increase pollution and damage the fragile polar habitat. At present, mining and drilling for oil are banned in Antarctica for at least the next 50 years. As the world's energy-hungry population grows, however, so does pressure on Earth's resources increase.

THE ANTARCTIC TREATY

The Antarctic Treaty

No one owns Antarctica, but, in 1959, twelve countries signed a document called the Antarctic Treaty, aimed at safeguarding Antarctica for the future. Today, forty-four countries have signed up. The Treaty, in summary, states :

- Antarctica shall only be used for peaceful purposes
- Scientists will have freedom to work in Antarctica
- Scientific information will be freely shared among all the countries with bases in Antarctica
- All territorial claims will be set aside
- Nuclear explosions and the disposal of radioactive waste are banned
- The Treaty applies to the land and ice shelves but not to the high seas

- All bases, ships, and aircraft operating in Antarctica must be open to inspection by any other Antarctic Treaty country
- People working in Antarctica must abide by the laws of their own country
- Treaty countries will meet regularly to discuss new ways of improving the Treaty
- Treaty countries will try to make sure that all activities are in keeping with the Treaty
- Any disputes will be settled by negotiation, or by the International Court of Justice
- If all countries agree, changes may be made to the Treaty at any time
- The Treaty is open to any member of the United Nations, or to other countries invited to join

Ice Cold

The landscape of the polar regions is dominated by ice. Because of the bitter cold at the Poles, the snow that falls on these areas rarely melts but settles in layers. The weight of each new layer presses down on the layers beneath, packing them down until they turn into ice.

Sheet Ice

Over 99 percent of Antarctica is covered by a gigantic ice sheet. The largest single mass of ice on Earth, it contains about 7,197,383 cubic miles (30 million cubic km) of ice and about 90 percent of the world's fresh water. The ice is so heavy that the underlying land has sunk below sea level beneath its weight.

This picture shows a selection of "growlers" — piano-sized pieces of ice floating in the sea. As with huge icebergs, the largest parts are submerged.

On average, the ice is 1.5 miles (2,450 m) thick. At its thickest, it reaches almost 3 miles (5,000 m) and is millions of years old. Most of the Arctic island of Greenland is also covered in a vast ice sheet up to 1.86 miles (3,000 m) thick. The ice sheet measures 1,553 miles (2,500 km) from north to south, and 621 miles (1,000 km) from east to west. It contains over 959,651 cubic miles (4 million cu km) of ice.

Glaciers and Icebergs

Under the force of gravity, ice from the center of the ice sheets flows toward the coast in frozen rivers called glaciers. In places, these float out to sea as massive ice shelves. Each year, thousands of chunks of ice break off the glaciers and ice sheets to form icebergs. They vary in size from relatively small "growlers" that are the size of pianos to towering bergs as tall as ten-story buildings. About nine-tenths of an iceberg is hidden underwater.

About 15,000 icebergs break off the Arctic glaciers each year, mostly from Greenland. Arctic icebergs are usually craggy and melt before they are two years old. Antarctic icebergs have flatter tops and are much bigger — the largest iceberg ever seen was the size of Belgium. They can survive for ten years or more. The wind and ocean currents can carry icebergs for thousands of miles (kilometers) from their source. Arctic bergs have been reported as far south as Bermuda.

Frozen Oceans

When the sea freezes, it forms a type of salty ice called sea ice. The Arctic Ocean is covered in a year-round layer of sea ice, between 16 and 22 feet (5 and 7 m) thick. The extent of ice cover varies with the seasons, expanding in winter and melting back in spring and summer. The sea around Antarctica is frozen for most of the year. The ice reaches its greatest extent in September, when it covers about 7,722,043 square miles (20 million sq km) of the Southern Ocean, more than doubling the size of the Antarctic. The ice is about 3.28 to 6.5 feet (1 to 2 m) thick.

Wind and waves keep the sea ice constantly on the move. These forces also break the ice up to form pack ice. Individual pieces of pack ice, called floes, range in size from a few yards (meters) to more than 6 miles (10 km) across. As the ice drifts, cracks and channels open up in it and the floes pile up on top of each other. Constantly changing ice conditions present great dangers for ships.

This cross-section of Antarctica shows the thickness of the massive ice cap (blue) that covers the area of solid land beneath.

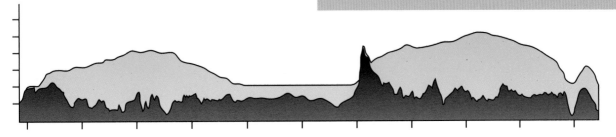

Animal Adaptations

Despite the harsh conditions, a surprising number of animals, birds. and plants are able to live in the polar regions. They have many special features and ways of behaving to help them survive the bitter cold and biting winds. Among these amazing animals are many that brave life on land or ice.

Ice Bears

Polar bears live along the Arctic coast and on the sea ice, where they often float for hundreds of miles (km) on ice floes.

These massive hunters are well adapted for life in the harsh Arctic climate. Their thick, oily fur helps to keep them warm and waterproof. A layer of blubber, or fat, underneath their skin adds extra warmth and

acts as a valuable food store when the bears' main food of seals is scarce. When there is little food about, the bears will also scavenge on whale, seal and walrus carcasses, and even steal food from human settlements.

Polar bears are usually solitary animals, except during the breeding season. In December or January, the female digs a warm den in the snow where her cubs are born. They stay in the den until spring, feeding on the female's rich, fatty milk.

Arctic animals, such as these polar bears, are specially adapted to the extreme conditions in which they live.

Cunning Camouflage

The adaptable Arctic fox changes its coat according to the seasons. In summer, it grows a thin coat of gray-brown fur. This color helps to camouflage the fox among the tundra rocks so that it can creep up unnoticed on its prey of small mammals and birds. In winter, the fox grows a thick white coat, which keeps it warm when it gets as low as –40° F (–40° C) and camouflages it against the snow. Another adaptation to the cold are the fox's small, round ears and nose. These help cut down on heat loss from the fox's body and make it less likely to get frostbite in these areas.

Antarctic Animals

Very few animals are able to survive all year round in the cold, dry, and windy climate of Antarctica. Many animals, such as penguins and terns (*see page 14*), are summer visitors who come to Antarctica to take advantage of the safe breeding sites along the coast and the plentiful food supplies that can be found in the Southern Ocean. Most of these animals leave again, however, when the hostile winter weather draws in. Only a few tiny insects and other invertebrates can live permanently on land. These include microscopic mites, worms, and springtails.

Antarctica's largest year-round residents are flightless midges, each just one-half inch (12 mm) long. These insects spend their lives hidden among the tangles of mosses and patches of gravel and wind-blown sand. They have developed an amazing range of techniques to stop their bodies from freezing in the bitter cold. They have a special chemical in their blood which acts like the antifreeze in cars. The females lay eggs which can survive the worst times of the year without care in case the adults die. The midges also lose all the water from their bodies and shrivel up when the temperatures fall. This prevents crystals of ice from forming in their fluids and damaging their body fluids and tissues.

One of the main reasons for the lack of land animals in Antarctica is the small number of plants. Plants start off almost all food chains, and animals cannot survive without them.

CARIBOU JOURNEYS

Caribou, or reindeer, visit the Arctic in summer when the weather is warmer and food there is plentiful. In the spring, huge herds of caribou travel along the same migration trails they have used for years, heading north to the Arctic tundra. Here, they feed on lichens and plants. Then, as winter approaches, they gather together to travel south once again to their wintering grounds in the northern forests.

For centuries, Arctic people, such as the Sami, have relied on these animals for food, fuel, and materials for making clothes, tents, and tools. Today, however, the caribou and their journeys are under threat as their habitat shrinks and oil-pipeline construction invades and destroys much of their traditional migration routes. Another danger is pollution, which is beginning to contaminate the lichen that the caribou eat.

Birds of the Poles

The Arctic tern makes a huge journey every year between the two Poles.

The polar climate is too harsh for many birds to survive there all year round. In summer, though, there are rich pickings to be had on the Arctic tundra and in the seas around Antarctica.

Many polar birds are summer visitors who travel long distances to feed in the Arctic and Antarctic regions. A great number of seabirds also come ashore to find places to breed.

Keeping Warm

Many polar birds share adaptations similar to those of polar animals. They are well protected against the cold, with dense, fluffy feathers and thick layers of fat under their skins. The ptarmigan is one of the few year-round residents of the Arctic tundra. It feeds mainly on leaves and berries. In winter, its pure white plumage hides it from predators among the snow. To keep warm, it burrows into the snow, hiding away from the biting wind. As summer comes, the ptarmigan changes color to brown so that it is still well camouflaged when the snow retreats and brown earth and grasses emerge.

Endless Summer

Each year, the Arctic tern makes a record-breaking journey to spend summer at either end of Earth. During the Arctic summer, it breeds around the shores of the Arctic Ocean. Then it flies south to Antarctica to take advantage of the rich summer food supplies. On each round trip, a tern flies nonstop for eight months and covers 25,000 miles (40,000 km). No other bird makes such a long journey. Most terns fly over the sea, feeding as they go. By making such a large migration, the tern spends most of its life in summer climes and daylight.

Winter Breeders

During the cold winter months, most birds leave the Antarctic and head for warmer places. The hardy Emperor penguins, however, breed on the ice in midwinter. The female lays a single egg, then spends the winter at sea. Meanwhile, the male incubates the egg, carrying it on his feet and tucking it warmly under a flap of skin.

For the next two months, in temperatures below –40° F (–40° C) with winds gusting up to 124 miles (200 km) per hour, the male cannot feed. For warmth, he huddles tightly with thousands of other male penguins. By the time the female returns to feed the chick, the male has lost half his body weight. Then it is his turn to go to sea and feed.

WANDERING ALBATROSS

Wandering albatrosses only come ashore to breed on isolated islands off the coasts of Antarctica. They spend the rest of their lives in flight. These amazing birds have wingspans of up to 11.48 feet (3.5 m), the largest of any bird. Their wings allow them to soar and glide on thermal air currents over the Southern Ocean as they search for fish and squid. Their beaks have razor-sharp edges and a hooked tip to help them fish. They can stay in the air for months on end, even sleeping on the wing. Using satellites to track the albatross' movements — a tiny satellite transmitter is fixed to a bird's body — scientists have found that an albatross can cover several thousand miles (kilometers) on a single feeding trip.

A colony of Emperor penguins with their chicks. Ungainly on land, the birds swim with ease underwater by using their flipper-like wings.

Polar Plants

At the polar regions, poor-quality, frozen soils and cold, biting winds make it tough for plants to grow. Most plants need water and sunlight for photosynthesis and cannot survive the lack of rain and long months of darkness at the poles.

These Antarctic rocks are covered with colorful lichens, which flourish despite harsh arctic conditions. Each thin patch of lichen can take hundreds of years to grow.

Despite the harsh conditions, some extremely tough and specialized plants have adapted to life at the Poles. These plants provide food for millions of insects, which spend the first part of their lives in the patches of unfrozen mud under the ice. Like the insects, the plants are also eaten by the large number of birds and mammals that visit the tundra during the summer months.

Arctic Plants

Over a thousand species of flowering plants live on the Arctic tundra. All of them grow low to the ground to keep out of the freezing wind. Tiny trees, like Arctic willows and birches, grow sideways along the ground for many yards (meters) but never become taller than ankle height. Arctic plants grow very slowly to save energy. Pencil-thin willow stems may be hundreds of years old.

In winter, the tundra may look bare and empty. As soon as spring comes, though, it bursts into life. To take advantage of the short growing season, many plants speed up their life cycles in spring and summer. While the weather is warmer and the days are longer and lighter, they flower very quickly and produce seeds and berries.

Antarctic Plants

Antarctica's extreme conditions mean that only the hardiest plants can live on land. Just two species of flowering plant survive on the Antarctic Peninsula. Yet over 400 species of lichen have been found in the few ice-free patches of rocks or ground. Lichens have various ways of coping with the darkness and cold of the polar regions. Some are black in order to absorb as much heat as possible from the small amount of light available throughout the year (*see page 5*). They also grow slowly, since there may be only a few days in the year when conditions are suitable for growth. It can take a lichen more than one hundred years to cover a patch of rock the size of a postage stamp. Some lichens can survive for over two thousand years.

The Antarctic ice sheet itself is almost bare, although some types of algae grow on the snowfields near the coast. The algae contain a red pigment that acts like a sunscreen to filter out the Sun's harmful ultraviolet (UV) rays and colors the snow pink. Some algae have tiny, thread-like structures for moving through the snow. They stop just below the surface, where they can collect the right amount of light to make food.

GONDWANA

Scientists have found fossils of tropical plants in Antarctica that show that it was once a much warmer place. Fossils of a conifer called *Glossopteris* have been found in Africa, Antarctica, South America, Australia, and India. Up until about 160 million years ago, these continents were joined together as part of a super-continent called Gondwana. Over the next 100 million years, Gondwana broke up and the continents moved apart and into their present positions. Antarctica slowly drifted towards the South Pole and got much colder. At this time, Antarctica's enormous ice sheets began to form, eventually covering the continent.

Life in the Polar Seas

Although they are very cold, the seas around the polar regions teem with life. In spring, as the ice starts to melt, vast numbers of tiny plants, called phytoplankton, bloom in the sea.

In spring, the loss of ice cover allows sunlight to reach the plants so that they can photo-synthesize. The water is also rich in nutrients that the plants need to grow. The plants are grazed by tiny animals, called zooplankton, which in turn are eaten by an astonishing variety of animals, from squid and other invertebrates to fish, seals, penguins, and whales.

In Cold Water

For animals that live in the polar oceans, keeping warm is vital. An animal's cells contain water. If this freezes, that stops the cells from working properly, damages tissues, and causes death. Beneath the pack ice, the sea stays unfrozen all year round and the temperature does not change much. Krill and other invertebrates that live in the sea are therefore protected from freezing — unless they get trapped in the ice. Fish are more at risk. Seawater freezes at about –28.76° F (–1.8° C); fish bodily fluids freeze at –30.02° F (–1.1° C). Many Antarctic fish have a chemical, like antifreeze, in their blood that lowers their freezing point to a safer 28.4° F (–2° C).

Giants of the Cold

The behavior of many animals is affected by the cold of the oceans and the fact that food is scarce for most of the year. Many of the invertebrates which live on the bottom of the Southern Ocean grow and move slowly to save energy. Some of these creatures reach

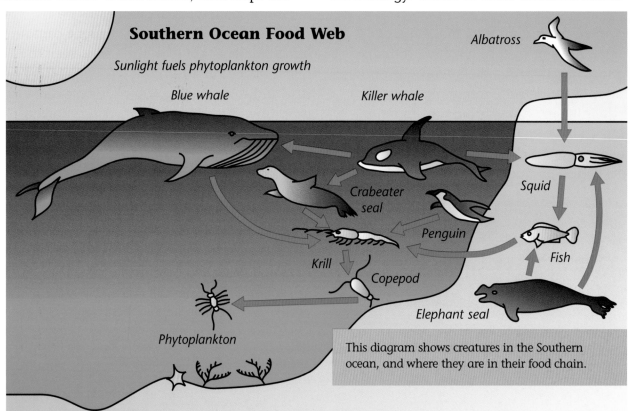

Southern Ocean Food Web

Sunlight fuels phytoplankton growth

Albatross

Blue whale

Killer whale

Crabeater seal

Penguin

Squid

Krill

Fish

Copepod

Elephant seal

Phytoplankton

This diagram shows creatures in the Southern ocean, and where they are in their food chain.

A DIET OF KRILL

Krill are shrimp-like crustaceans, found in huge swarms in the Southern Ocean. They play a crucial part in the Southern Ocean food web and are the staple diet of many fish, seals, birds, and whales. The krill feed on the tiny phytoplankton growing on the underside of the pack ice. It is estimated that the Southern Ocean contains about 441 million to 716 million tons of krill. Seals eat the most krill, about 143 million tons a year. Whales eat about 66 million tons. Krill is so important to the well-being of the Southern Ocean wildlife that scientists use radar and satellites to track and monitor the size and location of krill swarms. A drop in the amount of krill could cause starvation for many seals and whales.

an unusually large size. A relative of the common land-dwelling wood louse, the *Glyptonotus* is an Antarctic crustacean that scavenges for its food on the seabed. It grows up to 7.87 inches (20 cm long), which is over ten times as long as an ordinary wood louse.

A Seal's Life

Seals are well suited for life in the polar seas. They have streamlined bodies and paddle-like flippers for swimming, and thick layers of fat under their skin for warmth. The Weddell seal of Antarctica lives farther south than any other mammal in the world. Also one of the hardiest, it spends the winter under the ice, searching for fish and squid to eat. It gnaws breathing holes in the ice with its large teeth. Underwater, a seal can hold its breath for an hour and dive to depths of over 984 feet (300 m). In summer, the seal breeds on the sea ice and islands around Antarctica.

Weddell seals have a thick layer of insulating blubber beneath their skins to keep out the cold.

Poles under Threat

Today, the polar regions are under threat. Human activities, such as mining, drilling for oil, and overfishing, are putting pressure on the Poles and damaging these fragile habitats.

The landscape, people, plants, and animals of the Poles have existed side by side for many centuries. In spite of their harsh climates, both the Arctic and Antarctica are extremely sensitive environments. Even the slightest changes could upset the delicate, natural balance of the polar regions.

Global Warming

Many scientists now think that Earth is getting warmer because of the greenhouse effect. People are burning increasing amounts of fossil fuels, such as oil, gas, and coal, raising the amount of carbon dioxide in the atmosphere. Small amounts of carbon dioxide and other "greenhouse" gases, such as methane, occur naturally in the atmosphere. They play a vital role in trapping the Sun's heat, like the panes of glass in a greenhouse, and stopping it from escaping into space. Now, increases in carbon dioxide are making Earth grow warmer. Not all scientists agree. Some argue that Earth is now getting warmer because of natural changes in the climate.

Impact on the Ice

Many scientists predict that Earth's temperature may rise by about 3.6° F (2° C) by the year 2100. Even this small increase could have devastating effects. Already, the polar ice sheets are shrinking and some Antarctic ice shelves are breaking up. Many glaciers have started to melt and retreat. The pack ice around the Arctic is getting thinner. Some studies predict that the Arctic Ocean will be completely free of summer ice before the end of the twenty-first century. If the polar ice melted completely, sea levels would rise by 164 feet (50 m) or more. This would be catastrophic, causing the flooding of low-lying coastal communities around the world.

A minority of scientists argue that, instead of the ice melting, the opposite will happen. They say that if the climate gets warmer, the warm air will carry more moisture to Antarctica. This moisture will then fall as rain or snow and make the ice sheet thicker.

THE OZONE LAYER

In the 1980s, scientists in Antarctica discovered a huge hole in the ozone layer. This protective shield is a layer of ozone gas about 15.5 miles (25 km) above the Earth. It shields the Earth from the Sun's harmful UV rays, which can cause skin cancer and blindness in humans and kill animals and plants. Similar holes have also been found over the Arctic region and are being carefully monitored. The main cause of the problem are gases called CFCs. They are used in refrigerators, air-conditioning, plastic foam and aerosol sprays. Today, many governments have taken measures to ban CFCs. These gases take a long time to disappear from the atmosphere, so it will take another fifty to one hundred years for the ozone layer to recover.

Habitat Loss

If Earth's climate continues to warm and the polar ice continues to melt, much of the polar habitat will be lost — with terrible consequences for polar wildlife. If plants and animals cannot adapt to the changing conditions, they will die out. Polar bears, for example, travel vast distances on floes of Arctic sea ice when they go hunting for seals. Now that the sea ice is melting earlier in the year, the bears have less time for hunting and for building up the fat stores they need to survive the winter when food is scarce. The danger is that the bears will starve.

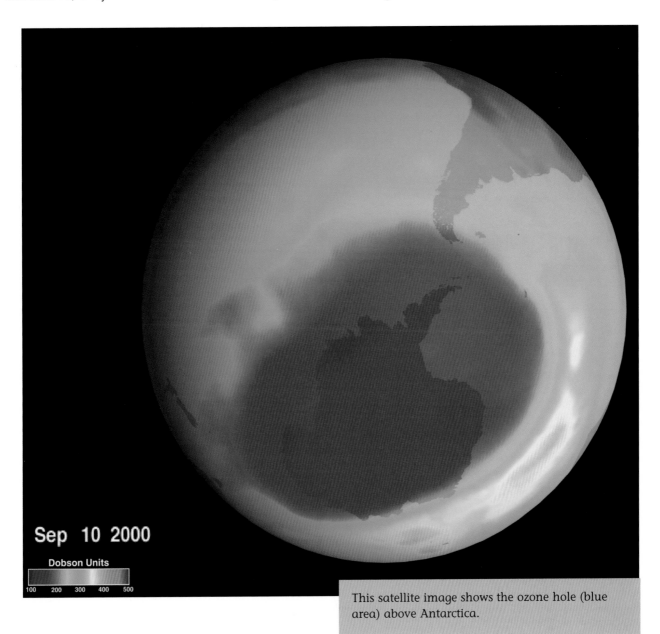

Sep 10 2000

Dobson Units

100   200   300   400   500

This satellite image shows the ozone hole (blue area) above Antarctica.

Drilling for Oil

Commercial mining is banned in Antarctica until 2041, but, in the Arctic, things are less protected. In the 1960s, oil was discovered at Prudhoe Bay in Alaska and the 808 mile-(1,300-km-) long Trans-Alaska pipeline was built to transport the oil to the port of Valdez. The region now produces about a fifth of the United States' oil, and oil companies continue to look for new supplies.

Recently, the U.S. government announced plans to drill for oil in the Arctic National Wildlife Refuge. Covering 7 million acres (3 million hectares) of northeast Alaska, the refuge is one of the last unspoiled areas of wilderness on Earth. It is home to huge herds of caribou and other species, including polar bears, wolves, and Arctic foxes. It is also an important stopover for many migrating birds. Environmentalists fear that drilling will damage this amazing habitat for ever. Roads, pipelines, airstrips, and power stations will have to be built, which will displace animals, damage plants, and disrupt the lives of local people.

Polar Pollution

Pollution is another major threat to the polar regions. In 1989, the oil tanker *Exxon Valdez* ran aground off Alaska, spilling 11 million gallons (38,800 metric tonnes) of oil into Prince William Sound. Hundreds of miles of coastline were drenched in oil, and thousands of seabirds, fish, and sea mammals were killed. It was one of the worst environmental disasters in the history of the planet.

Accidents have also happened in Antarctica. In 1989, a supply ship called the *Bahia Paraiso* struck rocks off the Antarctica Peninsula. Its cargo of over 500,000 gallons (11,904 barrels) of fuel leaked into the sea, forming a huge slick. The remote location made the clean-up campaign quite difficult.

Scientists studying the Arctic are also worried about the effect of pollution from factory chemicals and farm pesticides on local wildlife. These chemicals contaminate soils and seawater, poisoning the food chain. Rare beluga whales live in the Arctic Ocean. Already endangered, these whales are now under even greater threat. Many are dying

Building pipelines, such as this one in Alaska, can result in damage to the fragile Arctic ecosystem.

POLAR TOURISM

Every year, thousands of tourists head for the Poles to enjoy the breathtaking scenery and unique wildlife. Even though numbers are still low, tourists can threaten the fragile polar environment by leaving litter and disturbing wildlife habitats. If tourists get too close to penguins and other seabirds, they may upset birds' breeding and nesting patterns. Strict rules are now in place for tourists to follow in both the Arctic and Antarctic, and most tourists comply. Polar tourism is not all negative. When they return home, polar tourists can help improve general awareness of how precious the polar regions are.

A group of polar tourists land from an inflatable boat. What effects will tourism have in the future?

of cancer and it seems that deadly chemicals washed into the sea may be to blame. These are taken in by the invertebrates on which the whales feed.

Exploiting Ocean Resources

Among the most important natural resources of the polar regions are fish, squid, and krill. Millions of tons are caught each year by high-tech fleets, equipped with computers, satellites, and radar for locating fish. Strict limits have been set on the size of catches to prevent overfishing. Some fishing fleets, unfortunately, are breaking the rules. In the Southern Ocean, for example, huge numbers of the Patagonian toothfish are being caught illegally. Their oily, white meat makes them a valuable catch. The problem is that these slow-growing fish take thirty years to reach adult size. So many are being taken that the fish do not have time to breed, grow, and build up stocks again.

What Is Being Done?

A great deal of information remains to be discovered about how the polar regions work. Many scientists, conservation groups, and governments are working hard to learn more about the Poles. All agree that it is vital to protect these fragile habitats and their unique wildlife for the future.

Science in the Freezer

No one lives permanently in Antarctica, but thousands of scientists from all over the world travel there to work. They live mostly on research stations equipped with science laboratories, living quarters, kitchens, hospitals, libraries, and gyms. The scientists also spend weeks away from these stations on field trips. Many different types of scientific research are carried out. Glaciologists monitor the extent of the ice. Biologists study how wildlife adapts to the harsh climate. Geologists explore the land under the ice, and meteorologists carefully monitor weather conditions. Antarctica's clear skies also make it a perfect place for astronomy.

Many scientists work at research stations in the Arctic. These scientists generally focus on environmental issues, such as the effects of pollution and climate change on the region's local people and wildlife. Projects have included the International Tundra Experiment (ITEX), which investigated the possible impact of global warming on the plants of the Arctic tundra.

Studying the Ice

Because of concerns over climate change, glaciologists specialize in studying the polar ice. They use many cutting-edge techniques, such as ice-penetrating radar, lasers, and satellite images to monitor changes in the thickness and extent of the ice, and they also monitor changes in the height and speed of glaciers as they advance or shrink.

In the Arctic, submarines traveling under the sea ice have collected information about tens of thousands of square miles of ice, including data about its thickness and structure. Until recently, however, the Antarctic sea ice was

Scientists conduct polar research at remote stations such as this one in Antarctica.

Scientists are constantly searching for new approaches to their work. In 2003, a team of Norwegian and British researchers used a group of white whales to collect information from the Arctic Ocean. Because of the thick ice cover, it is difficult to monitor the area by ship. The whales dive to great depths of over 650 feet (200 m) to feed, so the scientists fitted sensors to the animals' backs. Each time the whales resurfaced, data from the sensors was sent by satellite to the researchers. Scientists are using the information to monitor the temperature of the water under the ice. This careful monitoring helps scientists track how much the Arctic is being affected by global warming.

Arctic glaciologists, working from a research ship, take ice samples for analysis.

largely unexplored. Then, in late 2003, a brand-new roving submersible, *Autosub 2*, was launched under the Antarctic sea ice. It fires sonar pulses upward to measure the thickness of the ice.

Ice Cores

The ice sheets over Greenland and the Antarctic have taken thousands of years to form. By drilling down into the ice and removing a core, scientists can tell how old the ice is. An ice core drilled recently in Antarctica was over 1.8 miles (3 km) long and the ice at the bottom almost one million years old. Ice cores are extremely valuable. Locked in the ice is a unique record of past climate change. As the ice forms, particles of dust or pollen get trapped inside. By analyzing these gases and particles, scientists can discover what Earth's climate and atmosphere were like in the past. The ice also provides information about past events, such as volcanic eruptions. The results help scientists predict how the climate might change in the future.

Whatever activities take place in Earth's polar regions, humans must make sure that equipment and materials such as these are removed afterward to prevent further damage to the fragile environments.

Conservation at Work

Environmental groups are working hard to save the polar regions. In the 1980s, the group named Greenpeace began a long-running campaign to protect the Antarctic region. Greenpeace was worried about the environmental damage caused by the scientific bases. Problems included dumping sewage and chemicals into the sea, burning garbage, and blasting wildlife sites to make room for buildings and airstrips. Thanks to pressure from Greenpeace, the bases have now cleaned up their acts. Many now have strict waste management programs and also specially trained environment officers. Their garbage is no longer burned or dumped in the polar regions but recycled or shipped home.

In the Arctic, the World Wildlife Fund (WWF) began its International Arctic Program in 1992 as a joint effort between the eight Arctic countries: Canada, Iceland, Greenland (of Denmark), Finland, Norway, Russia, Sweden, and the United States. Its aim is to protect the Arctic from further damage and to make the rest of the world aware of how important the region is. Among other things, the WWF is working to find ways of reducing pollution, saving local wildlife, and protecting the rights and culture of local Arctic people.

Saving Living Resources

In the nineteenth and early twentieth centuries, hunters came to Antarctica in search of whales and seals. Sealers came especially to hunt fur seals for their valuable pelts and elephant seals for their blubber. By the 1920s, both species were almost extinct. The whales of the Southern Ocean suffered a similar fate. As whale stocks were wiped out in other oceans, whalers moved further south.

Millions of whales were killed for their blubber, whalebone, and meat. In 1994, the International Whaling Commission (IWC) declared the Southern Ocean a whale sanctuary. Whales are now protected from commercial hunting, although a few are still caught for scientific research. Seals are also protected by the Convention for the Conservation of Antarctic Seals.

In both polar regions, certain areas have been set aside as protected parks. Home to polar bears, caribou, musk oxen, and many rare Arctic plants, the world's largest national park covers 375,291 square miles (972,000 sq km) of northeastern Greenland. Many seals, whales, and walruses live around the coasts.

New park reserves are being set up. In 2004, Australia established a fully-protected marine reserve in its Antarctic waters. Covering an area about one-and-a-half times the size of Switzerland, it includes a group of remote islands that are home to several threatened species. To safeguard these animals and their habitat, commercial fishing and exploration will soon be banned in the new reserve and only a limited amount of carefully-monitored scientific research will be allowed.

THE FUTURE

What does the future hold for the polar regions? Already, there are many treaties and measures in place to protect these amazing habitats. Should they remain protected areas set aside for peaceful, scientific research — or should they be developed like other parts of the world? Parts of the Arctic have already been developed, and the Antarctic may follow. Recently, scientists began calling for tighter rules to control the collecting of biological samples which could be used by commercial companies. These samples include a type of protein used by certain kinds of Antarctic bacteria as an antifreeze. It could be used to keep frozen foods fresher for longer, making the protein very valuable to food companies. In the Arctic, governments are trying to find ways of developing the region without causing more damage to the fragile ecosystem. As for the other end of Earth, many people believe that the best way to protect Antarctica is to turn it into a world park where all commercial activity is completely banned. Whether either of these plans will work remains to be seen.

Further Information

International Agreements
The Antarctic

In addition to the Antarctic Treaty (*see page 9*), four international agreements have been made to tackle environmental problems. Here are the main points of each agreement:

1. (1964) Agreed Measures for the Conservation of Antarctic Fauna and Flora (now updated in the Environmental Protocol)
   - Killing or catching any bird or mammal without a permit is forbidden
   - Permits will only be given for scientific samples and essential food
   - Vehicles and explosives must not be used near wildlife colonies
   - Some areas will be designated Specially Protected Areas
   - Non-indigenous species are not allowed without a permit
2. (1972) Convention for the Conservation of Antarctic Seals (CCAMLR)
   - Yearly catches are strictly controlled and reviewed regularly
   - Killing Ross and Antarctic fur seals is banned
   - Killing any seals between March and August is banned.
   - Killing any seals in special reserves is banned
3. (1982) Convention on the Conservation of Antarctic Marine Living Resources (CCAS)
   - Applies to fish, molluscs, crustaceans, and all other species which form part of the Antarctic marine ecosystem
   - Any harvesting of resources must follow strict conservation measures
   - Stocks must not fall below certain levels.
   - A balance must be kept between resources caught and those that depend on them for food
   - No long-term changes may be made to the marine ecosystem
   - Conservation measures must be followed
   - A special scientific committee will give advice about these measures
4. (1998) Protocol on Environmental Protection to the Antarctic Treaty
   - Sets aside Antarctica as a natural reserve devoted to peace and science
   - Sets out rules to protect the environment
   - Gives priority to scientific research
   - Bans all activities relating to mineral resources (apart from scientific research)
   - Bans non-indigenous species without a permit
   - Sets out rules for:
     -Environmental impact of activities
     -Conservation of flora and fauna
     -Waste disposal and mangement
     -Prevention of marine polution

The Arctic
The Arctic Council
The governments of the eight Arctic countries — Canada, Iceland, Finland, Denmark/Greenland, Norway, Russia, Sweden, and the United States — have joined forces to form the Arctic Council and are working together to protect the entire Arctic region.

Arctic Council Programs

The Arctic Council has created programs to safeguard the Arctic environment:

1. Arctic Monitoring and Assessment Program (AMAP) monitors pollution in the Arctic and looks at its causes and at its impact on the environment. Also looks at international agreements on pollution control.

2. Protection of the Arctic Marine Environment (PAME) looks at ways to prevent pollution of the Arctic marine environment from land- and sea-based activities, such as shipping, oil and gas exploration and extraction, and ocean dumping.

3. Conservation of Arctic Flora and Fauna (CAFF) aims to protect Arctic species and to regulate how they are harvested and used, to prevent overfishing and so on. It also looks at how climate change affects Arctic wildlife and how wildlife is adapting to the changes.

4. Emergency, Prevention, Preparedness and Response (EPPR) exchanges information about how best to prevent oil and chemical spills in Arctic waters and how to act quickly if a spill occurs.

5. The Arctic Climate Change Impact Assessment (ACIA) runs projects to assess how much the Arctic is warming up and the impact of future climate change on the region, on its wildlife, and on its people, and suggests corrective measures that may be taken to limit unhealthy climate change.

Web Sites

Here are a few Web sites to help you find out more about the polar regions:

astro.uchicago.edu/cara/vtour
Take a virtual tour of the U.S. McMurdo base in Antarctica, and return to this site's home page to link to a CIA map on territorial claims and research stations.

usarc.usgs.gov
The U.S. Antarctic Resource Center provides a huge collection of maps, photos, and information on the southern Polar region.

www.arctic-council.org
Discover more about the Arctic Council, which is made up of the countries that border the Arctic.

www.mnc.net/norway/roald.html
Learn about Roald Amundsen, the Norwegian who arguably won the honors — amid much controversy about his methods of feeding his men — of being the first man to reach the South Pole. He also, again controversially, was probably the first man to fly over the North Pole.

www.panda.org/about_wwf/ where_we_work/arctic/index.cfm
The WWF Arctic Program shares details of current Arctic projects, including tracking polar bears.

www.spri.cam.ac.uk
Visit the *Library* and *Archives* sections of the Scott Polar Research Institute Web site to learn more about the Arctic, its people, landscape, and wildlife.

Glossary

adapted
having certain features or ways of behaving which allow a plant or animal to survive in a particular habitat

albedo effect
the way in which dark colors absorb, or soak up heat, while light colors reflect heat away

algae
a group of simple plants, ranging from tiny, one-celled plants to huge seaweeds

Antarctic Circle
an imaginary circle drawn around the southernmost part of Earth

Arctic Circle
an imaginary circle drawn around the northernmost part of Earth

axis
an imaginary line drawn through the middle of Earth, between the North and South Poles

bacteria
microscopic, single-celled living things found almost everywhere on Earth

blubber
a thick layer of fat under an animal's skin

carbon dioxide
a gas found in the atmosphere that is released when fuel, such as coal or wood, burns and when animals breathe out

CFCs
gases, called chlorofluorocarbons, which are destroying the ozone layer above the Poles

crustaceans
animals, such as krill, shrimps, lobsters, crabs, and woodlice, which have exo-skeletons and two sets of antennae

dry valleys
areas of bare rock in Antarctica which are not covered in ice and snow

ecosystem
a community of animals and plants and the habitat in which they live

food chains
the way in which living things are linked together by what they eat

food web
a number of different food chains that are linked together for survival

geology
the study of Earth's structure and history

glaciologists
scientists who study ice, especially glaciers

ice cap
a vast perennial covering of ice over land

invertebrates
animals which do not have backbones or skeletons inside their bodies

lichen
a complex, plant-like organism formed by a partnership between an alga and a fungus, which typically grows on a flat surface, such as a rock

meteorologists
scientists who study weather and climate

migration
the journeys undertaken by some animals between different habitats at different times of the year, usually in search of food

nutrients
substances in food that plants and animals need to stay alive

ozone layer
a layer of ozone gas in Earth's atmosphere that protects living things from the Sun's harmful UV rays

photosynthesis
the process by which green plants make their food from carbon dioxide and water, using energy from sunlight

phytoplankton
microscopic, single-celled plants that drift in the sea and form the basis, or beginning, of the ocean food chain

protein
a naturally occuring, highly complex chemical substance that a living thing needs for healthy growth

sonar pulses
sound waves sent out and reflected off objects; used, among other things, to measure the thickness of the polar ice

tundra
areas of flat, treeless land around the Arctic Ocean and in Antarctica, among other places, where only low plants and lichens are able to grow

UV (ultraviolet) rays
harmful rays from the Sun that are invisible to the human eye. UV rays can cause cancer and blindness in humans and kill animals and plants.

wind-chill factor
the way in which the wind makes it feel colder than it actually is (the stronger the wind, the colder it feels)

zooplankton
tiny sea animals that graze on phytoplankton and form an essential part of the oceanic food chain

Index